Brazil

FERNANDO DE NORONHA

33°W

0 50 mi

100 km

4°S

ST PAUL'S ROCKS

27° 22'W

0 0.5 mi

1 km

0° 52'N

TRINIDADE AND MARTIN VAZ

29°W

0 5 mi

10 km

20° 30'S

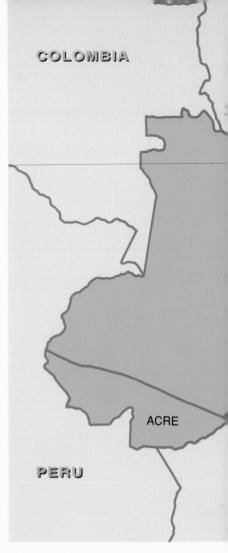

COLOMBIA

PERU

ACRE

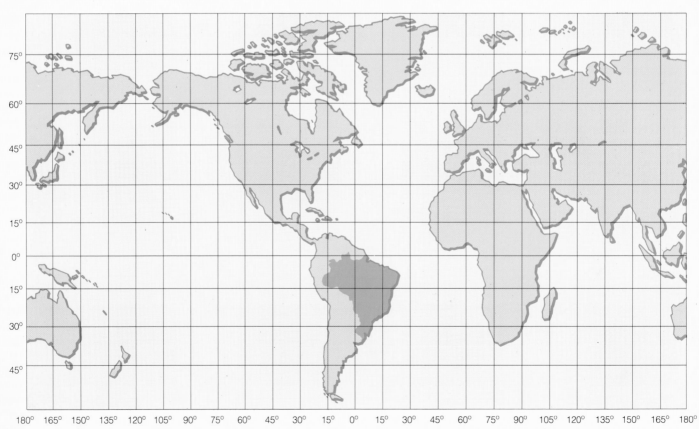

PACIFIC OCEAN

CHILE

Brazil

Marion Morrison

RAINTREE STECK-VAUGHN
PUBLISHERS

Austin, Texas

Published by Raintree Steck-Vaughn Publishers, an imprint of
Steck-Vaughn Company

Design	Roger Kohn
Editors	Diana Russell, Helene Resky
DTP editor	Helen Swansbourne
Picture research	Valerie Mulcahy
Illustration	János Márffy
	Coral Mula
Consultant	David Barrs
Commissioning editor	Debbie Fox

We are grateful to the following for permission
to reproduce photographs:
Front Cover: Magnum (Burt Glinn) *above*, Eye Ubiquitous/TRIP
(Julia Waterlow) *below;* Allsport, page 25 (David Cannon);
Colorific!, pages 16–17 (Claus C. Meyer); Sue Cunningham/Sue
Cunningham Photographic, pages 11 *above*, 18 *below,* 22, 23, 27
below, 29 *above,* 38, 43; Index/South American Pictures, page 12;
Roger Kohn, pages 34 *above,* 35 *right;* Tony Morrison/South
American Pictures, pages 8, 9, 11 *below,* 13, 14, 15, 16 *left,* 18–19,
20, 21, 24, 26, 27 *above,* 29 *below,* 31, 32, 33, 34 *below,* 35 *left,*
36, 37, 39, 41, 42; Zefa, page 30.

The statistics given in this book are the most up-to-date available at
the time of going to press.
Library of Congress Cataloging-in-Publication Data

Morrison, Marion.
Brazil / Marion Morrison.
p. cm. -- (Country fact files)
Includes bibliographical references and index.
Summary: Examines the landscape, climate, weather, population,
culture, and industries of Brazil.

ISBN 0-8114-1842-1

1. Brazil--Juvenile literature. [1. Brazil.] I. Title. II. Series.

F2508.5.M67   1994
981--dc20
93-26100
CIP
AC
Printed and bound in Hong Kong by Paramount Printing Group Ltd.

1 2 3 4 5 6 7 8 9 0 HK 99 98 97 96 95 94

C O N T E N T S

Words that are explained in the glossary are printed in
SMALL CAPITALS the first time they are mentioned in the text.

■ INTRODUCTION

Ask anyone what they know about Brazil, and most people will mention the Amazon River and the rain forest and its destruction, which has been popular in the news during the last few years. Others may say coffee, Carnival, and Rio de Janeiro's Copacabana Beach.

Most will mention soccer, for Brazil has won the World Cup three times, or Grand Prix racing since the recent triumphs of Nelson Piquet and Ayrton Senna. But although Brazil is well known for all these things, there is much, much more to this huge country.

Huge is the correct word, for Brazil is the fifth largest country in the world. Only Russia, Canada, China, and the U.S. have more territory. Brazil also has

◀ *Carnival involves over 20,000 dancers and lasts 2 days and nights in February or March. Here dancers in national colors celebrate Brazil's love of soccer.*

the fifth largest population in the world, but its population is not increasing as fast as most of the developing world. However, although Brazil is larger than the U.S., excluding Alaska and Hawaii, it has 95 million fewer inhabitants.

Brazil is the giant of South America. It is so vast that it shares frontiers with all except two of the other 12 countries that make up the continent of South America. (The exceptions

▼ *In rural Brazil there are many poor and unemployed. Outside this snack-bar in the northeast, people sell sweet corn cooked on a homemade metal grill.*

- Area: 3,286,470 square miles (8,511,996 sq km)
- Population: 1991: 153,322,000
- Density: 46 people per sq mile
- Capital and population: Brasília, 1.8 million
- Other main cities and population:
  São Paulo 9.7 million
  Rio de Janeiro 5.5 million
  Belo Horizonte 2.1 million
  Salvador 2 million
  Porto Alegre 1.3 million
  Recife 1.3 million
  Belém 1.2 million
  Manaus 0.9 million
- Highest mountain: Pico da Neblina, 9,896 feet (3,014 m)
- Language: Portuguese
- Main religion: Catholic
- Currency: Cruzeiro, written as CR$
- Economy: Increasingly industrialized
- Major resources: minerals, coal, oil, timber, rivers
- Major products: coffee, soybeans and soybean products, sugar, rubber, textiles, footwear, paper, motor vehicles, electrical and electronic goods, minerals
- Environmental problems: forest destruction and loss of plant and animal life; severe air pollution in São Paulo and nearby industrial towns; soil erosion

are Ecuador and Chile.) In industrial, economic, and political terms, Brazil is also the leader of the continent. After having relied heavily on agriculture for many years, Brazil is quickly becoming an industrialized nation. This gives Brazil a powerful position among the so-called Third World countries in their struggle to find equality with the developed nations of the world.

THE LANDSCAPE

Brazil covers nearly half the South American continent, crossed by the equator in the north and the Tropic of Capricorn in the south. From east to west, it covers almost the entire width of the continent, extending from the Atlantic Ocean to within 340 miles (550 km) of the Pacific.

The country is divided into five geographical regions, with 26 states. It includes several small islands. On the mainland, the most northerly region includes the Guiana Highlands, formed from ancient rocks and partly forested, where the two highest peaks in Brazil were found as recently as 1953. The Brazilian Highlands, a plateau area only 985–2,955 feet (300–900 m) high, broadly covers the center of the country. To the southeast lies the densely populated coastal strip, mostly just 328 feet (100 km) wide and backed by the steep Great ESCARPMENT, which was once covered with dense rain forest.

The other two regions are the area of the Amazon River to the north, and the TRIBUTARIES that lead to the Río de la Plata system in the south. Together they cover about three-fifths of the country.

▼ **Brazil is divided into four time zones. People in Manaus, 992 miles (1,600 km) up the Amazon, are one hour behind their friends in Belém, at the Amazon mouth.**

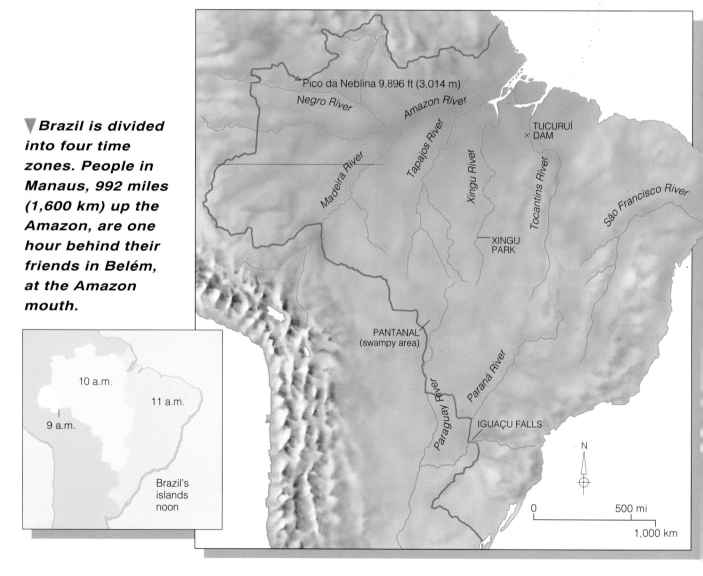

10 a.m.

11 a.m.

9 a.m.

Brazil's islands noon

Pico da Neblina 9,896 ft (3,014 m)
Negro River
Amazon River
Madeira River
Tapajós River
Xingu River
TUCURUÍ × DAM
Tocantins River
São Francisco River
XINGU PARK
PANTANAL (swampy area)
Paraguay River
Paraná River
IGUAÇU FALLS

N

0   500 mi
1,000 km

◄ *Much of the northeast is arid savannah, scrub forest, cacti and thorn bushes. Early attempts to raise cattle here failed because it is so dry. It has been called "one of the poorest places on Earth."*

KEY FACTS

● Brazil covers 47% of South America.

● Its Atlantic coast-line is 4,603 miles (7,369 km) long.

● Marajó Island is 15,000 square miles (38,850 sq km) and lies in the mouth of the Amazon. It is the world's largest island surrounded by fresh water.

● The São Francisco at 1,798 miles (2,900 km) is the longest river entirely in Brazil.

● The Amazon River has 17 tributaries more than 930 miles (1,500 km) long.

▲ *Brazil has many beaches and small natural coves, like this one on the stretch of coast between São Paulo and Rio.*

In the south many rivers that have their source in the highlands flow into the Paraná River and the Río de la Plata system, following rocky courses with falls and canyons until they reach level ground. The Iguaçu Falls, which are about 66 feet (20 m) higher than Niagara Falls, are on the Iguaçu River, a few miles from where it meets the Paraná River. The Paraguay River is

◀ *The Río Negro, a major Amazon tributary, has its source in the Guiana Highlands of northern Brazil. It meets the Amazon near the city of Manaus.*

▲ *The Amazon River is the world's second longest river.*

▼ *Amazonia, the area of South America through which the Amazon River flows, covers 2.9 million square miles (7.5 million sq km). It is almost as large as the U.S., as the comparison in this illustration shows.*

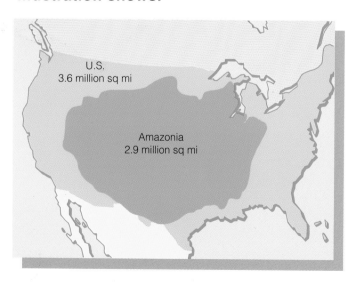

another tributary of the Paraná, flowing through an enormous area (54,054 square miles or 140,000 sq km) of level ground called the Pantanal that is a patchwork of lagoons, grassy plains, and trees.

Amazonia is the area of 2.9 million square miles (7.5 million sq km) in South America where the Amazon River and its 1,000 or more tributaries flow. Almost 2 million square miles (5 million sq km) of this land is in Brazil and is known to the Brazilians as "Legal Amazonia." It covers approximately 57 percent of the country and it is not all flat and covered with rain forest. In places it is hilly, even mountainous, and there are regions of grasslands, scrub forests, and swamps.

The main Amazon River flows from west to east, mostly within about 250 miles (400 km) south of the equator. The western section of the river in Brazil is known as the Solimões, and only the last 930 miles (1,500 km) to the Atlantic is called Amazon. This great river with its numerous side channels can be as much as 31 miles (50 km) wide. It narrows to

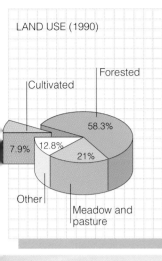

LAND USE (1990)

Cultivated

Forested

58.3%

7.9% 12.8%

21%

Other

Meadow and pasture

▼ *Much land in southern Minas Gerais has been cleared of its forests and is used for farming. This road leads to coffee plantations.*

about 1.2 miles (2 km) at Óbidos. Its mouth is 198 miles (320 km) across when it enters the sea.

In the region of Óbidos, rocky hills stand above the forest and are part of the very ancient foundation of South America. More of these hills extend across the northeast of Amazonia. The water of the tributaries in this region carries little SEDIMENT and is brown, due to rotting vegetation.

One Amazon tributary, the Madeira, is more than 2,046 miles (3,300 km) long. It is the world's longest tributary. Another, the Río Negro, rises in the far north and is more than 1,302 miles (2,100 km) long.

The true rain forest or "moist forest" extends in every direction around the Amazon River and is very varied. Sometimes the trees are giants of 165–200 feet (50–60 m), while others are spindly and only half as tall. Palms are abundant and in some places form extensive forests. Parts of the forest are frequently flooded, and the level of the river in the middle section may change by 50 feet (15 m) or more as rain swells the volume of the tributaries.

▶ *The Iguaçu Falls are on the Iguaçu River, on Brazil's border with Argentina. A total of 275 falls spill over a rocky precipice 200 feet (60 m) high, at a rate of 61,800 cubic feet (1,750 m³) a second.*

razil's climate and rainfall can be divided into five zones. Near the equator the temperature hardly changes. Abundant rain, averaging 98 inches (2,500 mm) a year, ensures a luxuriant forest growth that is believed to contain the world's richest BIODIVERSITY.

Immediately north and south of the equatorial zone the climate is tropical. There are two distinct seasons each year, a dry season and a wet season, with an average annual rainfall of about 60 inches (1,500 mm). The heaviest rains occur in summer (December to February). Both seasons are warm. The climate encourages the growth of grasslands, often with small, rather gnarled trees. This vegetation is known as CERRADO.

▶ *Most of Brazil has a tropical climate. It is cooler only in hilly areas and in the far south, which in winter sometimes has severe frosts.*

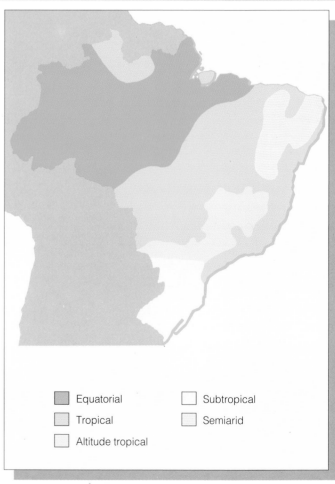

▢ Equatorial		▢ Subtropical	
▢ Tropical		▢ Semiarid	
▢ Altitude tropical			

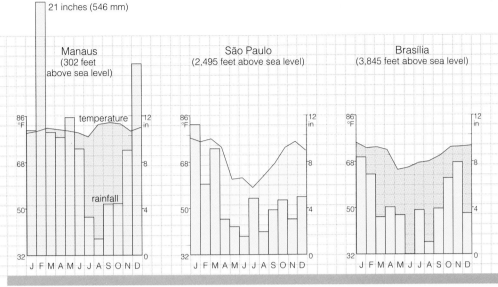

21 inches (546 mm)

Manaus
(302 feet
above sea level)

São Paulo
(2,495 feet above sea level)

Brasília
(3,845 feet above sea level)

temperature

rainfall

The Amazon city of Manaus, close to the equator, has a hotter climate and is much wetter than either Brasília in the central highlands, or São Paulo near the coast in the southeast.

In summer, when temperatures are over 40°C (104°F), everyone in Brazil heads for the beaches. Copacabana Beach is popular with Brazilians, but tourists prefer Rio's less crowded beaches, like Ipanema.

The northeast of Brazil is noted for its droughts and harsh climate. Annual rainfall is less than 40 inches (1,000 mm), and the temperature is always high, around 81°F (27°C). It is in this region (not the equatorial forests) that the hottest temperatures in Brazil have been recorded. The vegetation is the low scrub of sharply spined trees and cacti, called the CAATINGA. Here cattle are herded or roam semi-wild.

The southern states are cooler, with a greater range of temperature and distinct seasons. In some winters the frost can damage crops, and in the far south of the country snow may settle in midwinter. Heavy tropical storms occasionally strike the coastal region in summer, causing much damage.

Also cooler and subject to frequent winter frosts are tropical highlands, such as the hilly zone to the west of São Paulo and Rio de Janeiro. Here the altitude affects temperatures, which average between 64°F (18°C) and 72°F (22°C).

▲*Tropical rain does not last long but is so heavy that the streets can quickly flood.*

KEY FACTS

● Ninety-two percent of the country is in the tropics.
● The poorest part of the northeast, the SERTÃO, is hit by drought every 8 to 15 years and then suffers floods. In 1984 a 5-year drought ended in torrential rains that left 150 dead or missing and 700,000 homeless.

NATURAL RESOURCES

Brazil is immensely rich in natural resources, particularly in the states of Pará, Minas Gerais, and Rondônia. It was in Minas Gerais that the early explorers, the BANDEIRANTES, first discovered gold in 1693. Brazil's first gold rush followed this event. There have been other gold rushes since, one of the most recent in Serra Pelada in the Amazon.

Carajás, thought to be the world's largest iron deposit, was discovered in 1967. Today, Brazil is estimated to have a third of the world's iron ore reserves, which form the basis of its steel industry.

Other minerals in Brazil include coal, bauxite, manganese, zinc, nickel, lead, cobalt, cadmium, copper, chrome, and tin. There are reserves of gypsum, titanium, phosphates, and platinum, too. Deposits of niobium, thought to be the world's largest, have been found in Amazonas. Brazil also supplies 90 percent of the world market for several semiprecious gems, including amethysts and topazes.

Energy resources include large deposits of oil off the coast and in the states of Rio Grande do Norte, Sergipe, Bahia, and Ceará, and big gas reserves. Above all, there are thousands of miles of rivers, with potential for hydroelectricity. The Itaipú Dam on the Paraná River achieved the world's greatest output of hydroelectric power when the second stage was completed in 1990.

The country's timber reserves are estimated to be the world's third largest. Most of the wood is used as fuel, but

▶ *When gold was found in 1980 on Serra Pelada in Amazonia, within a month more than 10,000 gold prospectors rushed to the area.*

▼ *Carajás has the world's largest known iron-ore deposit. It also contains bauxite, manganese, and copper.*

softwoods, particularly paraná pine and eucalyptus, are grown in the south for local pulp and paper industries. Hardwoods from the rain forest include mahogany, which is used for furniture by countries like the U.S. and U.K. The felling and export of hardwoods has become very controversial and has caused considerable damage to the rain forests.

KEY FACTS

● The world's largest topazes and emeralds have both been found in Brazil.
● Brazil took its name from the brazilwood tree from which 16th century Portuguese settlers extracted a dye. It is one of 400 hardwoods found in the forests.
● Seventy-five percent of Brazil's oil reserves are offshore.
● In the late 1800s, latex from the Amazon tree *Hevea brasiliensis* was in huge demand for rubber goods.

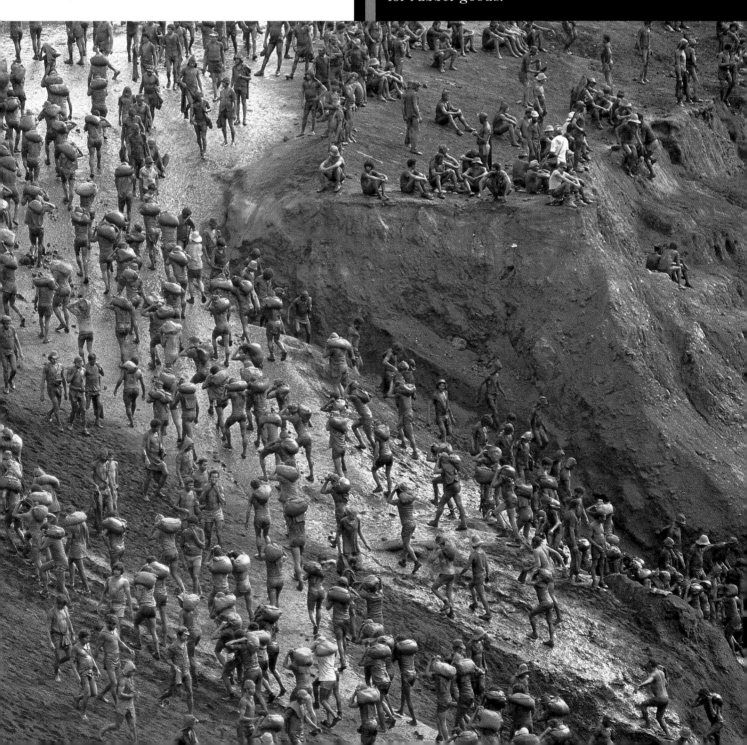

POPULATION

THE ORIGINAL PEOPLES

The native peoples of Brazil lived in the forests and along the rivers, hunting, fishing, and gathering fruits and nuts. When the Portuguese arrived early in the 16th century, it is estimated that there were between 1 and 2 million native Amerindian people. They were used as slaves, and many thousands died from diseases brought by the Europeans. Recently Amerindians have been exploited and killed as land speculators and highways go farther into the rain forest. There are probably less than 150,000 Indians now.

Although the Statute of the Indian Law of 1978 was meant to define Amerindian lands, many COLONISTS and ranchers ignore this. Some reserves, such as Xingu National Park, have been created, but

▲ *This crowd of people watching Carnival in Rio is made up of some of the different peoples that form Brazilian society. There are mestiços, whites, blacks, and mulattos.*

◄ *A Kayapo family. The Amerindian way of life is changing (notice the father's watch), but some traditional customs remain.*

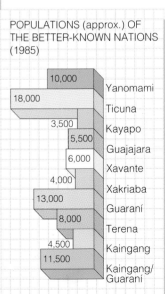

POPULATIONS (approx.) OF THE BETTER-KNOWN NATIONS (1985)

Population	Nation
10,000	Yanomami
18,000	Ticuna
3,500	Kayapo
5,500	Guajajara
6,000	Xavante
4,000	Xakriaba
13,000	Guaraní
8,000	Terena
4,500	Kaingang
11,500	Kaingang/ Guaraní

RACIAL MIX (1989)

Amerindians and Asians 0.5%
Whites 55.8%
Mixed races 36.8%
Blacks 4.8%

◀ **This diagram shows the different groups that make up Brazil's population.**

▼ **These two maps show how in 50 years, as the population has increased, people have moved near the coast, where the major cities are found.**

KEY FACTS

● The people of Rio are known as "Cariocas."

● Brazil's fastest growing city is São Paulo. Its population was 6 million in the late 1960s; today it is about 10 million.

● São Paulo has the world's largest Japanese community outside Japan.

● FUNAI is the state organization created in 1968 to protect the rights of the Amerindian peoples in Brazil.

increasingly Amerindian people are taking matters into their own hands, even using arms to defend themselves and their land.

BLACKS, MULATTOS, AND MESTIÇOS

Portuguese settlers developed vast sugar-cane estates in the Bahia region, and for 150 years these estates were the world's main source of sugar. To work the estates, the owners used slaves from Africa. Today there is still an African tradition in Brazil.

During the 400 years of Portuguese rule, marriages between Europeans and Indians, and Europeans and Africans, produced two new groups: the olive-skinned MESTIÇOS and the darker MULATTOS.

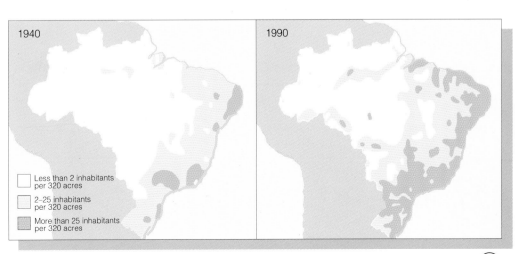

1940

1990

Less than 2 inhabitants per 320 acres

2–25 inhabitants per 320 acres

More than 25 inhabitants per 320 acres

IMMIGRANTS

Modern immigration began early in the 19th century. Only about 4.5 million foreigners, mostly from Europe, settled in Brazil after then. Most were Italians and Portuguese, but there were also Spaniards and Germans, and later Slavs from Poland, Russia, and the Ukraine, and Arabs from the Middle East. The Germans in particular, and some Italians, set up farms in the southern states of Santa Catarina, Rio Grande do Sul, and Paraná.

In this century the most significant immigrants have been Japanese. They have become the most prosperous ethnic group in Brazil, growing a fifth of the coffee, a third of the cotton, and all the tea.

INTERNAL MIGRATION

Traditionally the majority of Brazilians settled near the coast, but in the last 30 years the rapid movement from rural areas to urban centers has led to a very uneven distribution of the population. In parts of the interior there is an average of just two people per square mile. More than 75 percent of the people live in towns. Half of these are in just two cities: São Paulo and Rio de Janeiro.

People have moved from rural areas to the towns to seek work and better medical and educational facilities for their families. But the reality has been very different. Tens of thousands of people now live in shantytowns, or FAVELAS, on the outskirts of the cities, with little hope of ever getting a decent job.

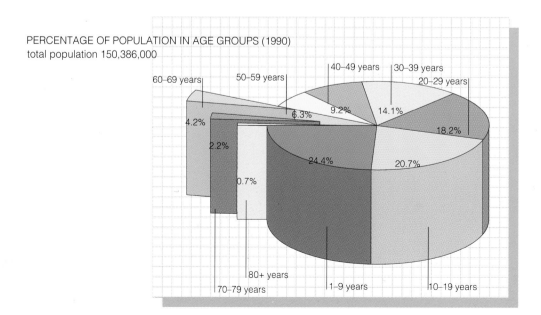

PERCENTAGE OF POPULATION IN AGE GROUPS (1990)
total population 150,386,000

60–69 years 4.2%
50–59 years 6.3%
40–49 years 9.2%
30–39 years 14.1%
20–29 years 18.2%
2.2%
0.7%
24.4%
20.7%
80+ years
70–79 years
1–9 years
10–19 years

◀ *A skyline of high rises in downtown São Paulo, Brazil's largest and fastest growing city. Founded in 1554, its population 100 years ago was 31,000, but then coffee planters began to move in. Today it has around 10 million people, with about 17 million in metropolitan São Paulo.*

▶ *The African tradition in Brazil is especially strong around the city of Salvador in Bahia, with colorful dress, rhythmic music, and exotic food all part of this culture. Here a Bahiana woman in traditional dress sells typical African-style snacks of* aracajes, *a bean dumpling fried in palm oil and mixed with dried shrimp and coconut milk paté.*

◀ *In the slums, or favelas, of Rio de Janeiro, home is often just one room.*

HEALTH STATISTICS	Brazil	U.S.	China	U.K.
Population estimate for 2025 (millions)	245.8	299.9	1,512.6	59.7
Urban growth,1990–1995 (%)	2.7	0.9	5.4	0.3
Percentage urban, 1990	75	75	33	89
Life expectancy in 1990 (years)	66	76	71	76
Death rate per 1,000	7	9	7	11
Birth rate per 1,000	26	14	21	14

▼ *About a quarter of the population of Rio de Janeiro live in favelas. Conditions are very poor, and often there is no water, light, or sanitation.*

FAMILY LIFE

Family ties are strong in Brazil. Three generations, including grandparents and young married couples, often live together in one house. Poorer families are frequently large, with five or six children, and grandparents look after the very young while the rest of the family work.

There is a wide gap between rich and poor. The wealthy live in luxury mansions or on vast estates, employ maids and gardeners, and enjoy the same consumer goods as any family in the developed world. Homes for the poor are shacks of cardboard and corrugated iron, furnished with the barest essentials and mostly without water, light, or sanitation.

EDUCATION

Attendance at primary school (age 7–14) is compulsory and free in state schools. There are also private, tuitional, and church-run schools. However, some 2 million children do not attend school — many because they have no school to attend. Less than a fifth

KEY FACTS

● Soccer player Edson Arantes do Nascimento (Pelé) has scored the most goals ever in a specified time: 1,363 between September 7, 1956 and October 1, 1977.

● Brazil has over 20,000 soccer teams.

● Divorce was legalized in 1977.

● In Brazil there are over 2,500 radio stations and 6 TV networks, of which TV Globo is the largest. There are no national newspapers because distribution throughout Brazil is too expensive. Most cities have their own newspapers.

● In 1990 there were 95 universities, of which 55 were run by the state.

POPULATION IN METROPOLITAN AREAS (1990)

17,112,712	São Paulo
11,205,567	Rio de Janeiro
3,615,234	Belo Horizonte
2,906,472	Pôrto Alegre
2,814,795	Recife
2,424,878	Salvador
2,119,774	Fortaleza
1,966,426	Curitiba
1,418,061	Belém

of all students go on to secondary school (age 15–18), and only a tiny percentage enter a university. Most schools are in urban areas, and these have better equipment and facilities than schools in rural regions.

Almost 20 percent of the population cannot read or write. This includes people who live in very remote areas or belong to Amerindian nations. Amerindian peoples have their own languages and often know little Portuguese, the official language of Brazil.

SOCIAL PROBLEMS

The extreme poverty in the urban slums, the high unemployment, and the increasing numbers leaving rural areas for the cities have led to serious social problems. The poorest people suffer most because the

▶ *Instead of going to school, many children work to earn money for their families. This young boy is helping to sort and pack fish for the market in Manaus.*

▲One of Brasília's most spectacular buildings is the circular cathedral, in the shape of a crown of thorns and surrounded by a moat. The interior (shown here) is below ground level.

▶Many Brazilians make pilgrimages to the statue of Padre Cicero from Ceará, who died in 1934. Local people regard him as a saint.

MAIN NATIONAL HOLIDAYS

January 1	NEW YEAR'S DAY
Feb/March	CARNIVAL AND GOOD FRIDAY
March/April	EASTER
April 21	TIRADENTES DAY
May 1	LABOR DAY
May/June	CORPUS CHRISTI
September 7	INDEPENDENCE DAY
October 12	PATRONESS SAINT OF BRAZIL
November 15	PROCLAMATION OF THE REPUBLIC
December 25	CHRISTMAS

state cannot provide for them, but children who live and work in the streets are particularly at risk. They may get involved in theft, robbery, or drug abuse. Brazil has a high murder rate, and many children have been victims of street violence.

LEISURE

Soccer is the favorite sport for most Brazilians. Rio's Maracanã Stadium is the largest in the world. Brazilians also make the most of their beaches, relaxing in the sun, playing ball games or water sports, and following fitness routines.

The greatest yearly event in Brazil is Carnival, which takes place in February or March. In Rio de Janeiro thousands of people, rich and poor, take part. They dance in the streets, wearing glittering costumes that take months to prepare.

▲ *The Brazilian soccer team that defeated Sweden 2–1 in the World Cup held in Italy in 1990. Brazil is the only country to have played in all 14 World Cup tournaments.*

RELIGION

About 90 percent of Brazil's population belongs to the Roman Catholic church. Other religions include the Protestant church, the Baha'i faith, and Buddhism.

The people of African descent still follow the religions of their ancestors. The main local religions are *Candomblé*, *Macumba*, and *Umbanda.* Priests and priestesses lead members in lively celebration of their gods.

The Amerindian peoples celebrate their own gods and spirits with music, song, and dance. They believe in spirits that live around them in the natural world.

Brazil became an independent country in 1822 when Dom Pedro I was crowned emperor. His son, Dom Pedro II, introduced many reforms. When Dom Pedro II passed the "Golden Law" to abolish slavery, the wealthy landowners became angry. They plotted with the military to depose him, and the empire ended.

Since 1889, when Brazil became a republic, there have been both military and civilian governments. One successful president was Getúlio Vargas (1930–1945 and 1950–1954), known as the "Father of the Poor" because of the measures he took to try and improve the welfare of the people. Another president, Juscelino Kubitschek, in 1960 founded the new capital city, Brasília, on an uninhabited plateau in central Brazil.

From 1964 until 1985, there was a military government, with political repression and torture of its opponents, but also economic success. The military eventually agreed to a new electoral college, which in 1985 voted in the first civilian president in 21 years. The Constitution was revised to ensure that five years later the next president was elected by the people. All persons age 18 to 69 who are literate must vote; those who are illiterate, over age 70, or between 16 and 17 years old may do so if they wish.

Two years after taking office in 1992 the new president, Fernando Collor de Mello, was forced to resign on corruption charges. Collor de Mello's fall shocked Brazilians.

Brasília is now home to the Congress building, ministries, president's office, and

In 1985 a civilian president was elected by an electoral college. By 1990, direct elections, with everyone able to vote, had been restored.

KEY FACTS

● Brazil has had 3 capital cities: first Salvador (until 1763), then Rio de Janeiro (until 1960), and now Brasília.
● Brazil was the last Western country to abolish slavery. In 1888, about 700,000 slaves were freed.
● Women were granted the vote in 1934.
● A year's military service is compulsory for all men age 18.
● In 1982 Mario Juruna was the first Amerindian to be elected senator.

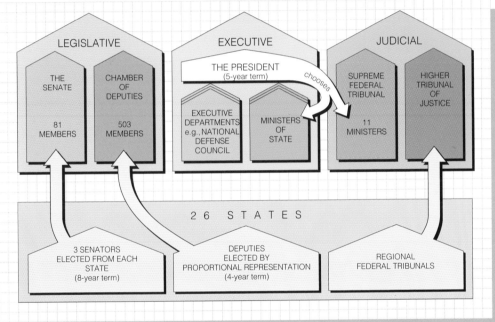

LEGISLATIVE		EXECUTIVE		JUDICIAL	
THE SENATE	CHAMBER OF DEPUTIES	THE PRESIDENT (5-year term) *chooses*		SUPREME FEDERAL TRIBUNAL	HIGHER TRIBUNAL OF JUSTICE
81 MEMBERS	503 MEMBERS	EXECUTIVE DEPARTMENTS e.g., NATIONAL DEFENSE COUNCIL	MINISTERS OF STATE	11 MINISTERS	

26 STATES

3 SENATORS ELECTED FROM EACH STATE (8-year term)	DEPUTIES ELECTED BY PROPORTIONAL REPRESENTATION (4-year term)	REGIONAL FEDERAL TRIBUNALS

▲ *The Congress building in Brasília is where the Chamber of Deputies and the Senate sit. It was designed by Oscar Niemeyer, Brazil's leading architect.*

▼ *Brazil's police force has to deal with a high level of theft and robbery.*

more than a million people. Congress is made up of the Chamber of Deputies and the Senate, who make the laws by which the country is governed. They are also responsible for financial policy and relations with other countries. The president needs approval from Congress for many acts, but he can veto laws passed by them. The 26 states and the Federal District elect their own governor and legislature, and each state is divided into MUNICIPIOS, each of which elects a mayor.

▲ *Brazil is governed by the president, Federal Senate, and Chamber of Deputies. The president and senators must be at least 35 years old, and deputies 21 years old.*

FOOD AND FARMING

Sugar, introduced in the 16th century by the Portuguese, was the first commercially successful agricultural crop in Brazil, followed early in the 18th century by coffee, brought in from French Guiana. Coffee grew well on the hilly uplands west of Rio de Janeiro and São Paulo, and in the southern states, where it has been concentrated since, though some is grown in the Amazon region, too. Today, Brazil is the world's largest producer and exporter of both sugar and coffee.

The south is Brazil's richest agricultural area. But farming lacks the advanced technology widely used in the U.S.

Throughout Brazil, only 20 percent of arable land is cultivated, and the agricultural industry employs less than a quarter of the working population.

Yet Brazil is almost self-sufficient in food production, except for wheat, and agricultural production accounts for about a third of exports. As well as coffee and sugar, major crops are soybeans, cocoa, cotton, tobacco, and corn. Rice, sorghum, and beans are grown for the domestic market. All kinds of fruits are plentiful, with some like *maracuja* or passion fruit now familiar in Western markets. Currently Brazil supplies 85 percent of the world market for orange juice concentrates. The forests also provide a range of nuts, of which the Brazil nut is the best known.

Although about a quarter of Brazilians live in the countryside, very few own their land. It is a major problem that 80 percent of the land is owned by just 5 percent of the population, and this has led to considerable violence between would-be settlers and gunmen (*pistoleiros*) hired by landowners. Opening up the Amazon has not proved to be the solution either. Colonists who received grants of land from the government have found it difficult to make the small farms profitable, and many have been forced to sell out to wealthy landowners or speculators. In addition, between 1985 and 1989, 350 people in the Amazonas were killed by *pistoleiros*. Ranching has met with little more success, again because the land is poor. In some places, 60 acres (25 ha) are needed to support just one cow.

The main center of Brazil's cattle industry, which overall contributes some 10 percent to world trade, is in the south and to a lesser extent in the northeast. Cowboys

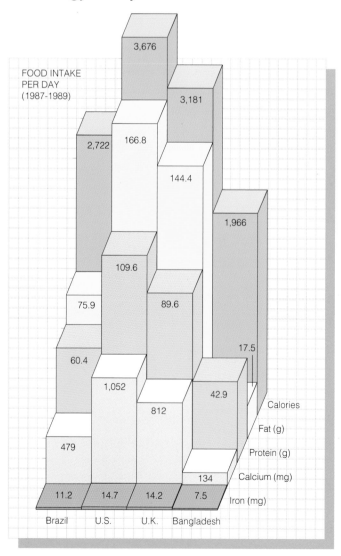

FOOD INTAKE PER DAY (1987-1989)

	Brazil	U.S.	U.K.	Bangladesh
Calories	2,722	3,676	3,181	1,966
Fat (g)	75.9	166.8	144.4	42.9
Protein (g)	60.4	109.6	89.6	17.5
Calcium (mg)	479	1,052	812	134
Iron (mg)	11.2	14.7	14.2	7.5

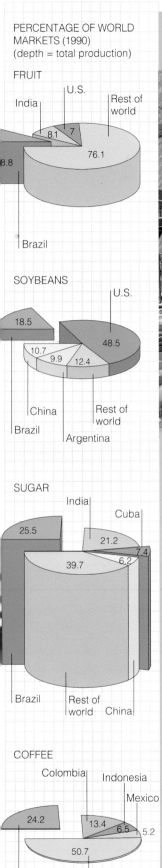

PERCENTAGE OF WORLD
MARKETS (1990)
(depth = total production)

FRUIT

India | U.S. | Rest of world
8.1 | 7 | 76.1
8.8
Brazil

SOYBEANS

U.S.
18.5
48.5
10.7 | 9.9 | 12.4
China | Rest of world
Brazil
Argentina

SUGAR

India | Cuba
25.5 | 21.2 | 7.4
39.7 | 6.2
Brazil | Rest of world | China

COFFEE

Colombia | Indonesia
Mexico
24.2 | 13.4 | 6.5 | 5.2
50.7
Brazil | Rest of world

▲ *Brazil is a major world producer of fruit, much of which is grown for export. Local market stands are always well stocked with fresh produce. Fruit in Brazil is inexpensive.*

▶ *The coffee picking season in Minas Gerais is from May to July. The coffee beans are then dried, sorted, washed, and bagged before being transported to the docks at Santos, ready for export.*

KEY FACTS

● The largest Amazon catfish, the piraiba, can grow to more than 10 feet (3 m) long and 5 feet (1.5 m) around the body, weighing about 440 pounds (200 kg).
● The world's largest shrimp bank is found in the mouth of the Amazon.
● Seventy-five percent of all Brazilian wine comes from the southern state of Rio Grande do Sul.
● Between November 1991 and October 1992, Brazil exported 20,349,000 sacks of coffee, each holding 132 pounds (60 kg).
● Brazil is a leading world producer of tobacco, and more than three-quarters of the crop is grown in the state of Bahia.

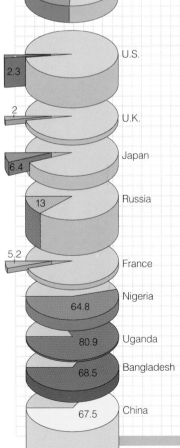

PERCENTAGE OF PEOPLE
EMPLOYED IN AGRICULTURE
(1990)   (depth = work force)

24.3	Brazil
2.3	U.S.
2	U.K.
6.4	Japan
13	Russia
5.2	France
64.8	Nigeria
80.9	Uganda
68.5	Bangladesh
67.5	China

▲ *Cowboys in Brazil leading a herd of zebu cattle, raised for the beef industry. As a breed, they survive well in dry and harsh areas.*

▶ *A small area of tropical forest remains here in southern Brazil. The remaining forest has been cleared to make way for cultivation. Contour farming follows the line of the low hills.*

known as GAUCHOS herd the millions of cattle that roam the vast grasslands of the south. They wear flat black hats and baggy trousers called *bombachas*. Their favorite drink is herbal tea, or *mate*. In contrast, the cowboys of the northeast, the VAQUEIROS, wear leather hats and trousers to protect their legs from the spiny scrub and cacti of the arid *caatingas*.

Although it has the longest continuous coastline in the world, Brazil has only a small fishing industry. Much of the catch is for the home market, and it is caught by local village fishermen. Off the northeast coast, fishermen use boats called JANGADAS, which traditionally were made of logs lashed together. Today most are manufactured from plastic tubing.

Food in Brazil varies according to the region. In cattle country in the south, huge quantities of meat are always available, while in the northeast the African-style Bahian dishes are mostly based on fish. Shrimp, crabmeat, or whitefish, mixed with coconut milk, *dende* oil from a palm, nuts, and spices, and served with rice, manioc, or cornmeal, make a truly exotic dish.

The national dish of Brazil is FEIJOADA. This meal is traditionally eaten on Saturdays and lasts for many hours. It consists of black beans, various types of dried and smoked meats – these can include ordinary cuts of pork or beef, but also pigs' feet and beef tongues – fried manioc flour, and rice. Other side dishes include fresh oranges and dried kale.

TRADE AND INDUSTRY

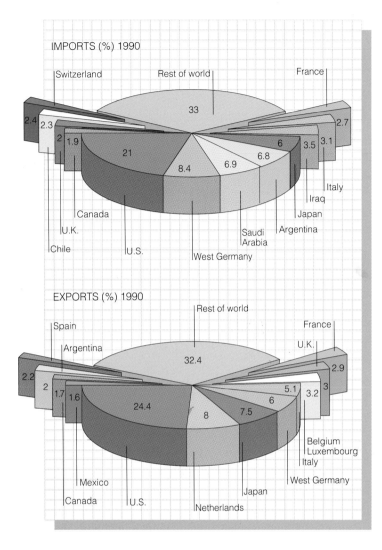

IMPORTS (%) 1990

Switzerland
Rest of world — 33
France

2.4
2.3
2
1.9
21
8.4
6.9
6.8
6
3.5
3.1
2.7

Canada
U.K.
Chile
U.S.
West Germany
Saudi Arabia
Argentina
Japan
Iraq
Italy

EXPORTS (%) 1990

Spain
Rest of world — 32.4
France
U.K.

Argentina

2.2
2
1.7
1.6
24.4
8
7.5
6
5.1
3.2
3
2.9

Mexico
Canada
U.S.
Netherlands
Japan
West Germany
Belgium Luxembourg
Italy

DEBT AND INFLATION

Since World War II, industry has taken over from agriculture as the basis of Brazil's economy. Billions of dollars have been spent on industry, first in the 1950s and then in the 1970s when the "Brazilian miracle" took place that transformed Brazil into an industrial nation. The generals who were in charge in the 1970s borrowed vast sums from international banks, which paid for the "miracle" but left the country big debts. Today Brazil has the largest foreign debt of any country in the world. Repaying it is an almost impossible task for a developing nation, even though Brazil in recent years has seen its exports exceeding imports.

Brazil has also suffered from high inflation, with prices of food and other goods increasing almost daily. Between 1986 and 1990, the currency was altered three times: in 1986, 1,000 cruzeiros was reduced to equal 1 cruzado; in 1989 the cruzado was replaced by the new cruzado; and in 1990 the new cruzado was replaced

▲*Brazil trades more with the U.S. than with any other country.*

▶ *Mahogany felled in the south of the state of Pará is cut and stacked ready for export from Belém, at the mouth of the Amazon.*

The Itaipú Dam was begun in 1975 and began generating electricity in 1984. It is 624 feet (190 m) high, its walls are 542 feet (165 m) thick, and a lake was formed behind the dam that covers 118 miles (190 km).

- In 1990 about 1 million tourists visited Brazil.
- The country's international debt in 1992 was estimated at $125 billion.
- Brazil's major ports are Santos (São Paulo), Rio de Janeiro, Paranaguá, Recife, and Vitória. Santos and Rio handle about half of all cargo.
- Brazil makes more than 1 million cars every year.
- With the creation of Itaipú Dam on the Paraná River for hydroelectric power, Sete Quedas, the world's largest waterfall (in volume) disappeared.

by the cruzeiro. With each change the value of Brazilian money has declined, and it is the poor people and lower paid workers who have suffered most.

MANUFACTURING INDUSTRY

One aspect of the "Brazilian miracle" was the development of manufacturing industries. State-run companies were established to run important industries, such as oil, steel, communications, and electricity. Foreign companies were invited to set up in the country, and large-scale industries were established for the construction of ships, vehicles of every kind, and aircraft. The vast majority of

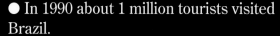

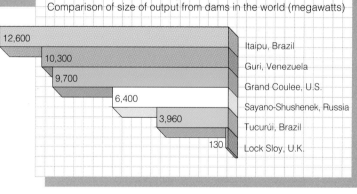

HYDROELECTRICITY (1991)
Comparison of size of output from dams in the world (megawatts)

12,600	Itaipu, Brazil
10,300	Guri, Venezuela
9,700	Grand Coulee, U.S.
6,400	Sayano-Shushenek, Russia
3,960	Tucuruí, Brazil
130	Lock Sloy, U.K.

consumer items used in Brazil, such as washing machines, refrigerators, televisions, and other household goods, are now manufactured there.

Technologically-based industries also developed, with demand for electronic and computer equipment, but traditional

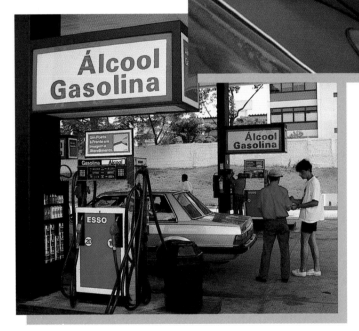

▼ *Alcohol distilled from sugarcane is sold from pumps alongside gasoline in most fuel stations. The majority of cars made in Brazil are adapted to use* alcool.

▲ *Of all the cars made in Brazil, the VW "beetle" was for many years the most popular. In cities it was used as a taxi. It was also suitable for rough rural roads.*

industry is heavily concentrated in the southeast, around the cities of São Paulo, Rio, and Belo Horizonte.

MINERALS AND MINING
Brazil is now beginning to realize the potential of its immensely rich mineral resources. International banks and organizations have helped to develop the Grande Carajás iron-ore mine and to build a new 552-mile (890-km) long railroad through the forest to a specially constructed new port near São Luis.

Brazil is a major exporter and producer not only of iron, but also of bauxite, from which aluminum is extracted, and in 1991 it was the world's leading producer of cassiterite, the mineral from which tin is

products, such as textiles, clothing, and processed food and drinks, are still important. Most shoe stores in the U.S. sell a range of Brazilian-made shoes, while Brazilian aircraft are used commercially in other countries. Timber has become more important, with softwoods used locally for paper and hardwoods felled for export.

Industry now accounts for about 70 percent of total exports and employs about a quarter of Brazil's work force. Most

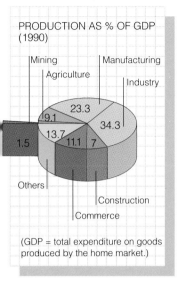

PRODUCTION AS % OF GDP
(1990)

Mining

Agriculture

Manufacturing

Industry

9.1

23.3

34.3

1.5

13.7

11.1

7

Others

Construction

Commerce

(GDP = total expenditure on goods
produced by the home market.)

◀ *Brazil's economy used to be based on agriculture. This chart shows how industry and manufacturing goods have overtaken agriculture and now represent almost 60% of the nation's output.*

made. There are also substantial gold reserves in the Amazon region.

ENERGY

The potential for hydroelectric power in Brazil is enormous, and it already provides more than 90 percent of the nation's electricity. The Itaipu Dam, built jointly by Brazil and Paraguay on the Paraná River, is now in its second stage. Its output of 12,600 megawatts is the largest in the world. Other such large projects include Tucuruí in the Amazon, and a proposed dam on the Xingu River that is planned to have an output of 17,000 megawatts.

In an attempt to reduce the expensive import of oil, in the 1970s and 1980s the government sponsored a project to use sugarcane alcohol as the basis of a new fuel, *alcool*. This was very successful. Of all cars sold in Brazil in 1984, 85 percent were alcohol-powered. As the price of imported oil has dropped, this project has been cut back, and Brazil has begun to develop its own oil reserves. It is now the third-largest oil producer in Latin America and by 1993, expects to be totally self-sufficient.

◀▲ *Two of Rio de Janeiro's best known landmarks are the statue of Christ on Corcovado (Hunchback) Mountain, and the Sugar Loaf Mountain at the entrance to Guanabara Bay. The statue is 131 feet (40 m) high, weighs 1,260 tons, and was completed in 1931.*

TRANSPORTATION

For centuries the most reliable way of traveling in Brazil was by river. Most freight and passengers now go by road or air, but rivers are still an important communication link in some remote areas, and oceangoing ships still travel to Manaus, 992 miles (1,600 km) up the Amazon. Santos, 39 miles (63 km) from São Paulo, is now the busiest of Brazil's ports, handling 30 percent of all cargo.

Some railroads were introduced in the 19th century, mainly connected with mines, but in the country as a whole there are few railroads for general passenger travel.

A dramatic increase in road building over the last 30 years has now linked Brasília, in the heart of the country, to most outlying areas. The first of the Amazon highways connected Brasília to Belém at the mouth of the Amazon River, while the most recent links the west of the Amazon to the industrial southeast, providing a route along which much of the newly felled timber is carried to the coast. The most ambitious current project is the 3,100 miles (5,000 km) Trans-Amazonian Highway from Recife in the northeast to the Peruvian border. Roads now carry 60 percent of the country's freight and 95 percent of passenger traffic, much of them on Brazil's excellent long-distance bus service.

The greatest problem in Brazil is its sheer size. Air transportation has transformed

KEY FACTS

● There are 26,660 miles (43,000 km) of navigable rivers in Brazil.
● Varig, Brazil's major airline, is the largest in South America.
● Both Rio de Janeiro and São Paulo have underground railroad systems. They each consist of two lines and operate every day except Sundays.

▼ *The floating dock in Manaus harbor was designed in 1902 to cope with the annual rise and fall in the river's water levels. It is connected to street level by a floating ramp.*

► *Varig is the largest Brazilian airline. The other main companies are Transbrasil, VASP, and Cruzeiro do Sul. Together in 1990 they transported about 17,049,000 passengers.*

PERCENTAGE OF ROADS PAVED (with tarmac, asphalt, or concrete surface)		TOTAL ROADS IN MILES (km) 1988		NUMBER OF CARS (1988)	
8	Brazil	1,037,714 (1,673,733)	Brazil	14,995,800	
56	U.S.	3,864,651 (6,233,308)	U.S.	140,655,000	
73	Russia	983,578 (1,586,416)	Russia	12,500,000	
100	U.K.	218,421 (352,292)	U.K.	21,347,700	

► **Part of the Trans-Amazon Highway, cut through the Amazon rain forest. Highways in Amazonia are expensive to build and to maintain. Many are not paved and can be very difficult to travel in the rainy season.**

communication over very long distances. There are regular services on major routes between main cities and frequent flights to remote, outlying regions where small planes can land on grass landing strips, or if necessary amphibian planes alight on the rivers. But for many people, flying is an expensive way to travel.

Older forms of transportation, such as horses and carts, are still much in use on rural areas. Water buffalo and carts are used in Marajó Island. However, many more people are riding bicycles and, if they can afford them, motorcycles that can cope with dirt roads and are fast.

THE RAIN FOREST

Brazil has more than a quarter of the world's rain forest and about a tenth of all known plant and animal species. Scientists admit that they still have much to learn about the Amazon rain forest. Several of the animals there, such as the tapir, capybara, and many species of monkey, exist only in Central and South American forests. Even now, previously unknown mammals are still being discovered, and the botanical finds seem limitless.

"Legal Amazonia" covers almost 60 percent of Brazil. Yet in 1960 only about 2 million people lived there, out of a total population of more than 70 million. In the 1960s thousands of people in Brazil moved from rural areas in the northeast and from the south to live in overcrowded city slums.

▲ *In February 1989 the Kayapo organized a meeting in Altamira to protest against planned development in the Amazon. Amerindians from all over Brazil met together there.*

▶ *The Brazilian government estimates that the rate of destruction of the rain forest in Legal Amazonia has fallen from 8,300 square miles (21,500 sq km) per year between 1978 and 1988 to 5,353 square miles (13,818 sq km) between 1989 and 1990.*

So many people needing homes and facilities put great pressure on cities like São Paulo and Rio de Janeiro, and it seemed to be an obvious solution to move them to the Amazon region. Since then, governments have looked to the region for

DISTRIBUTION OF THE WORLD'S
RAIN FORESTS (1989) (%)

Brazil | Others

27.5 | 23

49.5

Burma, Colombia, India, Indonesia,
Malaysia, Mexico, Nigeria, Thailand, Zaire

RATES OF DEFORESTATION (1990)

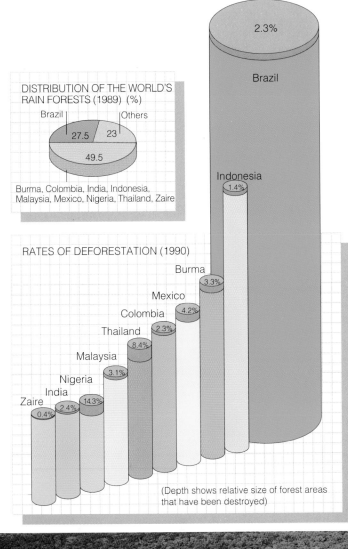

2.3%

Brazil

Indonesia
1.4%

Burma
3.3%

Mexico
4.2%

Colombia
2.3%

Thailand
8.4%

Malaysia
3.1%

Nigeria
India
14.3%

Zaire
0.4%

2.4%

(Depth shows relative size of forest areas
that have been destroyed)

*The hyacinth macaw is one of many
Amazon birds on the endangered list,
which also includes the jaguar. Several
species are already extinct.*

an answer to some of Brazil's social and economic problems. By doing so, they have opened up the area to settlers who destroy the environment with chain saws, shotguns, and garbage.

DESTRUCTION OF THE FOREST

Cutting highways through the forest was the first stage of the operation. Then people were offered money and land to settle there, but they soon realized that the land was not as fertile as it seemed. Almost all the forest's richness is in the trees. When they are cut down and burned, the valuable ash left behind is a good fertilizer for a few years but is soon washed away by the tropical rain. Any bare ground quickly hardens or is eroded by water and becomes unusable.

Commercial interests have also been responsible for destroying large areas of the forest. Although the Carajás iron-ore project has created little disturbance at the mine itself, much damage has occurred as people have settled along the railroad line. Some Amerindians have had to move from their land. A further threat to the environment has come from small-scale iron-ore smelters around the mine that are fueled by charcoal made from wood cut from the forest at a rate of more than 386 square miles (1,000 sq km) a year. The nearby Tucuruí Dam and other hydroelectric projects have led to further destruction.

The discovery of new gold deposits in the Amazon has led to thousands of gold-diggers, or *garimpeiros*, invading the sites. They damage the rain forest, pollute the rivers with the mercury that they use to separate the gold from the earth, and threaten the existence of Amerindians who stand in their way. The discovery of diamonds, tin, and gold in Yanomami territory has led to them losing a third of their land.

In their search for mahogany and other hardwoods, loggers often destroy many acres of other trees. Estimates of the extent of damage to the rain forest vary greatly, but in Brazil's Legal Amazonia 8.5 per cent (160,232 sq mi) have so far been cleared. However, recent satellite photographs show

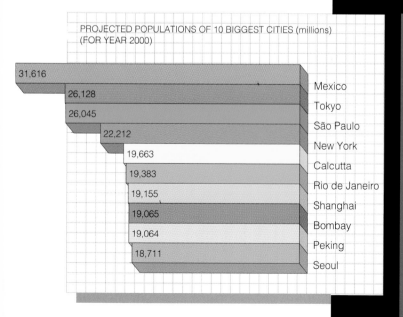

PROJECTED POPULATIONS OF 10 BIGGEST CITIES (millions) (FOR YEAR 2000)

City	Population
Mexico	31,616
Tokyo	26,128
São Paulo	26,045
New York	22,212
Calcutta	19,663
Rio de Janeiro	19,383
Shanghai	19,155
Bombay	19,065
Peking	19,064
Seoul	18,711

KEY FACTS

● The Amazon is thought to contain about 3,000 species of fishes.

● At the end of 1992, 2 cities in the Amazon, Belém and Manaus, each had a population of over 1 million.

● The first European expedition to explore the length of the Amazon lasted from 1541 to 1542.

● Scientists estimate that a patch of typical rain forest of 2.5 square miles (6 sq km) contains different species of 1,500 flowering plants, 750 trees, 400 birds, 150 butterflies, 100 reptiles, and 60 amphibians. Insects are too numerous to be counted.

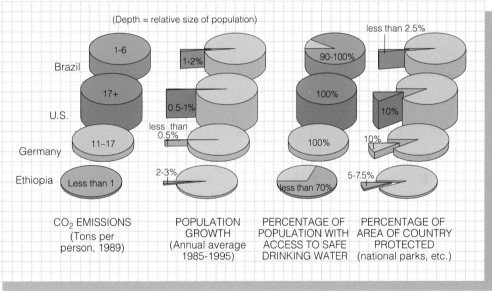

Cubatão, between Santos and São Paulo, was one of the world's most polluted places. In 1984 a gasoline pipeline laid across a swamp leaked, and 90 people died when their homes caught fire. Since then, the industries have invested in pollution control.

(Depth = relative size of population)

	CO₂ EMISSIONS (Tons per person, 1989)	POPULATION GROWTH (Annual average 1985-1995)	PERCENTAGE OF POPULATION WITH ACCESS TO SAFE DRINKING WATER	PERCENTAGE OF AREA OF COUNTRY PROTECTED (national parks, etc.)
Brazil	1-6	1-2%	90-100%	less than 2.5%
U.S.	17+	0.5-1%	100%	10%
Germany	11–17	less than 0.5%	100%	10%
Ethiopia	Less than 1	2-3%	less than 70%	5-7.5%

that since the late 1980s destruction of the Amazon forest in Brazil has been reduced.

THE GREENHOUSE EFFECT

Many people are concerned that burning the forest contributes to global warming, or the greenhouse effect, which is changing weather patterns. One reason for this warmth is increased carbon dioxide in the atmosphere, released from burning trees.

However, the burning of the Amazon forest added less than 2 percent to the world's carbon dioxide in 1991, while pollution from cars and industry in the U.S. added more than 22 percent. Concern is now turning more to the continuing loss of the Amazon rain forest and its great variety of unique animal and plant species.

In 1992 Brazil was host to the Rio '92 Earth Summit, attended by more than 100 heads of state. The agenda included a plan to limit carbon dioxide emissions and a proposal to preserve the world's great biodiversity, which was agreed to by almost every country except the U.S.

Brazil has recognized its special place in the environment and unveiled an environmental program for the Amazon region in 1989. It has also set aside regions, such as part of the Pantanal and large areas of Amazonia, as wildlife parks and reserves.

Many Brazilians are very aware of the dangers to the environment, and one city in the south is trying hard to show us how to prepare for the future. Curitiba is Brazil's "green city." There, children are taught to recycle their garbage. Traffic flows smoothly along clear routes, and special bus lanes are marked in central areas. Parks are plentiful and tended well, and flowers are everywhere.

It has been estimated that in less than 30 years São Paulo and Rio de Janeiro will be two of the most populated cities in the world. Yet overall Brazil's population growth is relatively low. But if there is to be a more equal distribution of the population, future governments will need to find ways to persuade people not to leave rural areas. This problem may be helped as the cities and towns farthest from Rio and São Paulo are developed, with their own airports and bus terminals, so that people see less reason to move to the coast in search of better facilities.

◀ *Children in Brazil's "green city," Curitiba, are encouraged to take an interest in their environment. This is a drawing class in which the topic for the day is the rain forest.*

KEY FACTS

● Quinine, from the bark of the cinchona tree, is used to treat malaria. To date, only 1% of rain forest plants have been studied, but scientists believe there are many other plants that could be used for medicines, perfumes, dyes, insecticides, foods, fuels, oils, and other purposes.

● It is estimated that by the year 2025, Brazil's population will have increased from 153 million (1991) to almost 250 million.

Other problems that must be faced are the increasing gap between rich and poor, the huge international debt, and the need to redistribute land so that the majority of the population can benefit. However, in many ways Brazil is a very fortunate country, and compared with many others, it can look forward to an exciting 21st century. Backed by its enormous natural resources, it is well placed to become a leading industrial and political force. It has also shown that it is well aware of its responsibility to look after the environment for future generations.

► *At the Earth Summit held in Rio de Janeiro in 1992, workmen put the finishing touches to a golden tree of life, shaped like a globe, a symbol for the future.*

FURTHER INFORMATION

BRAZILIAN CONSULATE GENERAL
3810 Wilshire Boulevard, Los Angeles, CA 90010

CHILDREN'S RAIN FOREST
P.O. Box 936, Lewiston, ME 04240

ENVIRONMENTAL DEFENSE FUND
1616 P Street NW, Washington, D.C. 20036

RAINFOREST ACTION NETWORK
450 Sansome, Suite 700, San Francisco, CA 94111

BOOKS ABOUT BRAZIL
Ashford, Moyra. *Brazil.* Raintree Steck-Vaughn, 1991
Bailey, Donna and Sproule, Anna. *Brazil.* Raintree Steck-Vaughn, 1990
Bender, Evelyn. *Brazil.* Chelsea, 1990
Carpenter, Mark. *Brazil: An Awakening Giant.* Macmillan Child Group, 1988
Cross, Wilbur. *Brazil.* Childrens, 1984

GLOSSARY

BANDEIRANTES
Literally "flag-bearers." They were soldiers of fortune from São Paulo who explored and opened up the interior of Brazil in the late 17th century.

BIODIVERSITY
A new word describing the many different animals and plants living together in one habitat

CAATINGA
A Brazilian name for a thorny sparse forest, particularly in the northeast of Brazil

CERRADO
A Brazilian name for an area of grassland and low trees. (It comes from *campos cerrados*, meaning "closed fields.")

COLONIST
A settler, or planter. The Portuguese word *colono* is widely used in Brazil.

ESCARPMENT
An inland cliff, or steep slope

FAVELAS
Slums in Brazilian cities

FEIJOADA
The national dish of Brazil, made from black beans and smoked meats

GAUCHOS
The cowboys of the southern grasslands of Brazil

JANGADAS
Traditional fishing boats used in the northeast of Brazil

MESTIÇO
A Brazilian of Portuguese and Indian descent. Also known as *pardos*, the *mestiços* now make up a large proportion of Brazil's working population.

MULATTO
A Brazilian of European and African descent

MUNICIPIOS
A town or urban community

SEDIMENT
Matter, such as rock or soil, that falls to the bottom of a river

SERTÃO
Arid land in the northeast of Brazil

TRIBUTARY
A river or stream that flows into a main river

VAQUEIROS
The cowboys of the northeast region of Brazil

INDEX

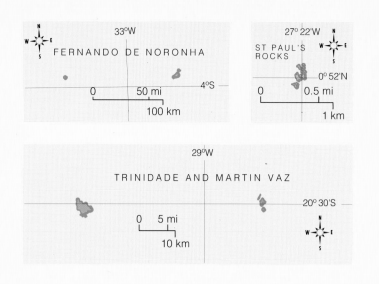

FERNANDO DE NORONHA

33°W

0   50 mi

100 km

4°S

ST PAUL'S ROCKS

27° 22'W

0   0.5 mi

1 km

0° 52'N

TRINIDADE AND MARTIN VAZ

29°W

0   5 mi

10 km

20° 30'S

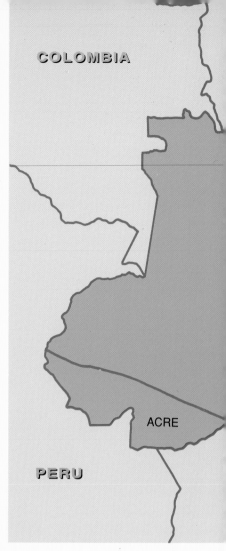

COLOMBIA

PERU

ACRE

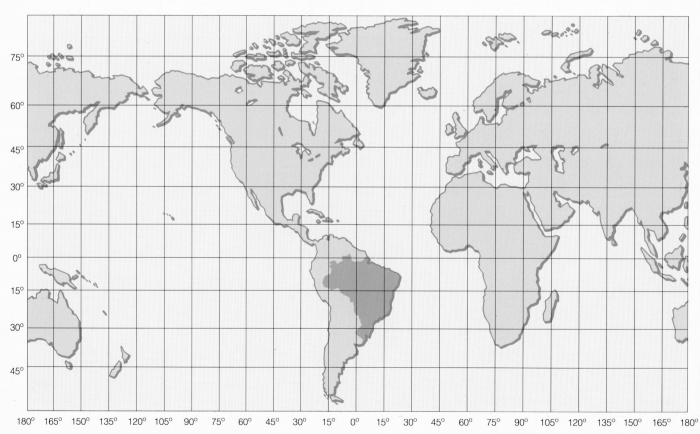

75°
60°
45°
30°
15°
0°
15°
30°
45°

180° 165° 150° 135° 120° 105° 90° 75° 60° 45° 30° 15° 0° 15° 30° 45° 60° 75° 90° 105° 120° 135° 150° 165° 180°

PACIFIC
OCEAN

CHILE